Gift to:

_____

From:

_____

Date:

_____

I hereby give this spiritual guide to you. May this book deepen your Personal Relationship (PR) with God and help you discover the greatness I see in you! I am excited to hear and celebrate your victories in your growth throughout your journey!

The Gratitude Awakening Practice

A Daily Practice To Discovering Your Greatness.
Dr. Angel Jackson

Honey Tree Publishing, LLC
Louisville, Kentucky 40215
www.honeytreepublishingus.com

Copyright © 2021 by Dr. Angel Jackson
ISBN: 978-0-578-30046-7
First Edition- 2021 (paperback)

All rights reserved. No part of this book may be used or reproduced in any manner whatsoever without written permission, except in the case of brief quotations. For information address Honey Tree Publishing, LLC. All scriptures are from the New Living Transition and The Message (MSG) translations of the Bible.

Library of Congress Cataloging-in-Publication Data
Jackson, Angel, 1985- The Gratitude Awakening Practice: A Daily Practice to Discovering Your Greatness

Cover Art by: Brandon Jackson
https://www.thehealingtent.org/our-team
Interior Design by: Honey Tree Publishing, LLC

Printed in the United States of America

In Harmony

To my village, thank you for always reminding me of the importance of going inward.

Thank you for showing me the value of serving and giving back to the community.

Your continued efforts of faithful actions towards yourself and others have allowed many to grow and discover their greatness.

To my ancestors your dedication and commitment to our family and community are not forgotten. It will forever flow through me.

In Harmony.

To every person who is committed to discovering and giving greatness to themselves and others… I write this book for you.

Let love and light be your guide to the elevation of becoming your highest self.

Acknowledgments

With gratitude, I would like to thank God for giving me the gift of writing and allowing me to spread greatness to others. I would not be who I am if I did not do the work of having a Personal Relationship (PR) with God.

Next, I would like to thank my Mr. Magnificent for being open to growth personally and as a union to discover our true beauty in this world. Our light together is magical, and I cannot express how blessed I am to have you with me on this divine journey called life. To my two children that bring love, laughter, and light daily to me, I adore you, Emerald and Braxton. I am blessed to be your mother and I do not take the gift lightly.

To my amazing, foundational, and strong village, Mom and Dad, I appreciate you all dearly. Thank you for being YOU and always being open to me growing and being the best version of myself. To my brother George, I am so proud of who you are and how much you continue to grow and elevate. I am excited to witness the expansion of your family and see how much love and light they will bring to you and this world.

Last, but certainly not least, I cannot express enough gratitude to my grandparents, bonus parents, aunts, uncles, cousins, friends, and day ones! I am so thankful that you all have expressed so much support to me throughout the years and how you all have shown me the importance of enjoying life, serving others, and never taking yourself too seriously (so enjoy life to its fullest)!

A Note from the Author

"Just Breathe"

  The sounds of life are constantly around you. Small and big voices full of laughter and joy. The sounds of chirping birds and dogs barking from a close residence. Let's not take into account the *soulistic* sound of music bellowing nearby. While the sound of nature is blissful, a natural sound that is often taken for granted is your breathing. Having the ability to take a deep breath in and releasing it out is a blessing. When you are able to take a moment to stop and focus on your breath, you can draw closer to the life, peace, and stillness that is inside of you. When you stop to "Just Breathe" you will begin to reflect on the inner work and steps to enhancing your best self.

  I must admit that there will be distractions that await you in this world that can cause you to not set aside personal growth for yourself and unapologetically dive deep into growing your Personal Relationship (PR) with yourself and God. That is when having a daily spiritual practice is key. This work comes when the world is completely silent, without distractions, and when the only sounds you hear are your breath with the stillness of energy around you and the flow of serenity allowing you to "Just Breathe". In order to do that, my friend, you must be willing to have an open mindset to personal growth.

  The GAP, or the Gratitude Awakening Practice, is a daily spiritual practice that allows you to discover your greatness and show greatness to others. Through the GAP, you have the ability to acknowledge and exercise the following five energy shifting tools: **Gratitude, Respect, Encouragement, Appreciation, and Time.**

  Throughout this book, I provide you with interactive GAP Reflection Questions and Exercises to help you track your thoughts and perspectives. Before you continue through this book, take 5 minutes to reflect on the below questions:

GAP Reflection Questions:

- How often do you take time to focus on your breath?

- How often do you take time to acknowledge that every day is an opportunity to live/choose life?

- How often do you take a moment to express gratitude for yourself and appreciate the moments to "Just Breathe"?

Table of Contents

Introduction	1
Chapter 1: Creating the Space	4
Chapter 2: The GAP (Gratitude Awakening Practice)	7
Chapter 3: The ART (Achieving Revolutionary Transformation) of Releasing Greatness	17
On Your Mark, Get Set and Reset!	18
The "Shed Effect"	21
Release	23
Unlocking Your Great Box	25
Set the Space and Pace	27
Self-Reflection	28
Respect	32
Prayer	36
The Dynamic Duo of Gratitude and Appreciation	39
Meditation	42
Rest to Reset	46
Time	50
Practice	50
Conclusion	54

The GAP: A Quick Reference Sheet

The GAP Mindful Pace/Steps
1. Setting Up the Space
2. Intentional Breathing
3. Daily Affirmation
4. Daily Prayer
5. Daily Journal of Self-Reflection
6. Daily Reading
7. Daily Meditation

Five Foundational Tools
1. Practice
2. Meditation
3. Prayer
4. Self-Reflection
5. Release

(GREAT) Energy Shifting Tools
1. Gratitude
2. Respect
3. Encouragement
4. Appreciation
5. Time

Introduction

For over fourteen years, I have encouraged people from all walks of life to expand on their PR (Personal Relationship) with God. Throughout my life, many women and men would ask, "How did you survive the storms in your life?" Some would even ask, "How did you have the strength and courage to go after your dreams, exercise, write books, co-found a ministry and still have time for your husband and children?" The questions that many people pose are thought-provoking to the point that I eventually reply with a smile, "It is how I start my mornings and how I end my nights." I believe that how we start our morning sets the tone and foundation for the day. I also believe that how we end our evenings allows our mind to rest and cultivate for the next day, allowing us to be our best selves.

While many may believe that this practice is a challenge, I believe there is no such thing as a challenge. There are only opportunities for growth and understanding. As you read this book, allow yourself to be open to growth and understanding; know that it is okay to not be perfect; trust that you are resilient; be mindful of your selection of words and thoughts to yourself; accept your authenticity; and understand that the process takes time. You have to be willing to enhance your spiritual practice and have a greater understanding of who you are and who God has called you to be. The GAP (Gratitude Awakening Practice) will require you to be uncomfortable which will allow you to stretch, strengthen, and heal. During this uncomfortable phase, you will find yourself becoming more flexible in areas where pain and strain once lived. These areas will begin to loosen from your acute ability to acknowledge your greatness!

You are great, and you have the ability to show and give greatness to others. For this to transpire, the GAP will require you to go deep within yourself more than you ever have. I know you can do it and I believe you will! This journey called life is long, but with God, He can provide you with the tools to enjoy and conquer the days ahead with tranquillity, enlightenment, joy, discernment, and patience. When this practice is used with daily intention, implementation and stillness can help profoundly transform your life. When you are willing to enrich your life, there will become enlightenment which will therefore produce elevation. By taking action, you will create an awakening in your daily practice that will put you on a quest to discover, deepening your level of knowledge and application with these Five Foundational Tools, which are **Practice, Meditation, Prayer, Self-Reflection,** and **Release**. When you activate these tools, it will allow you to experience acceleration, elevation, and transformation in your thought process and walk with God, therefore, growing your Personal Relationship (PR) with God. When you discover your personal greatness, it will require you to give greatness to others. By utilizing these Energy Shifting Tools throughout your life, you will be able to give and show **Gratitude, Respect, Encouragement, Appreciation,** and **Time** to others and yourself. When you are in the flow of greatness your awareness of life will be heightened exponentially! So, the question that I ask is, are you ready for greatness?

    While seeking elevation and growth, it is critical to your well-being and self-exploration that you do not rush the process. I will say it again. Do not rush the process. For my people in the back, repeat after me... Do not rush the process. Alrighty, we are all here now, focused and ready to listen. Think about it this way. Anything worth exploring and working towards takes time. Every intricate detail of growth requires you to examine all aspects of your life. That is why you must continue with the GAP. There will be times when it will be difficult to stay on course and set aside PR time. There are going to be times when you do not feel like getting up early and or setting aside time for you to just breathe and grow. But, you must continue to push towards elevation. Practice is practice. Simply said. You cannot get better at anything without practice. This devotional will provide you with the tools to draw closer to God and to discover more of your true self. It will allow you to create a space dedicated to The GAP and allow you to follow *The ART of Releasing to acknowledge your Greatness*. Throughout this book, there will be scriptures, reflection questions, and reflection exercises to allow you to meditate on your spiritual awakening practice.

The GAP will require you to be uncomfortable. At times, you will feel unsure if you need to practice the Five Foundational Tools (**Practice, Meditation, Prayer, Self-Reflection,** and **Release**). But, that is because you are doing something that is new. Your mind, body, and spirit will require some adjustments as they are not used to operating in a creative conception. By tapping into your creative conception will spark an emotional response to inspire you to take action on your purpose and discover your greatness. Other times, The GAP will require you to be flexible with yourself and gentle with your thoughts and the process. Give yourself some grace. Realize that you are here because of His grace. Be kind and gentle with yourself. Speak kind words to yourself. Love the image of you and understand that there is only one of you. This transformation will be something like none other than you have ever experienced.

This experience was life-changing for me and that is why I decided to write this book to inspire people all over the world to set aside time for God, to be intentional about self-discovery, and to open up to their true authentic selves. I want people across the entire planet-- West Coast to East Coast-- to know that they have a voice. That they can do the unachievable and unimaginable. *Why*? Because they have purpose and they are able to move mountains and create masterpieces. All people are great and capable of diving deep into their personal greatness. Therefore, enjoy the gifts and tools God placed in you.

GAP Reflection Questions:

- *What are two strengths that you appreciate about yourself? How can you leverage those two strengths to enhance your daily life?*

Chapter 1
Creating the Space

In The GAP, it is essential to create the space to expand and elevate your spiritual, mental, and overall growth. It is vital that you incorporate and embed a personal practice. When you use various tools such as **Practice, Meditation, Prayer, Self-Reflection,** and **Releasing**, it gives you the ability to flow throughout the day. You are able to combat more challenges and create solutions that will motivate you to be more creative. Therefore, allowing you to be a profound person holistically. Think about it, we all are striving for greatness in our own way. However, this goal requires us to step outside of our comfort zone and try something new. Our minds are more powerful than we often recognize. When you are willing to open not only your mind but, more importantly, your heart, it allows for a purposeful transformation to take place. The more we set our intentions on the matters of the heart, we can heal from the matters of the world.

Releasing past mistakes, guilt, or actions is not for others to do. It is for you to acknowledge and understand that we all make mistakes. It is your responsibility to release the past of yesterday and to release your greatness for today. Each day is set and when you start with the Gratitude Awakening Practice or GAP, it creates new grace, mercies, and blessings for you to experience and enjoy. But, you have to be open in your heart, mind, eyes, ears, and spirit to truly see it. Every day, we have the ability to encounter a multitude of laughter, smiles, and peace. When you set your intention on the matters of the heart, you will begin to discover the everyday joys of living.

We have to work together with God and therefore grow more in discovering who God has called us to be. The GAP allows us to have an impactful Personal Relationship with God. We all have gifts and talents and a special calling designed and unique to us. We can't let what others believe or dictate what our gifts are. We must trust ourselves in knowing that if this gift was placed in our heart, mind, and spirit, then it is there for a reason. Nothing happens by coincidence. Understand that God has a purpose for your life. That is why it is worthwhile to set aside time to understand your journey to identifying and understanding how to operate within your gifts and talents.

Our gifts are like making wine. Reflect on the process of making wine, for instance. It starts off as a grape. That grape goes through a process called fermentation. According to Chris Russell, "During fermentation, yeast- our microbiological friends convert grape sugars into alcohol. There's a lot more than just alcohol production going on, though. Fermentation drives complex chemical reactions that affect the flavor, aroma, and even color of the finished wine." That grape has to go through various stages before you can experience that delightful glass of wine. But the beautiful thing about the process of winemaking is that there are different types of wine with different flavors. There is a multitude of wines and vineyards, and not one is alike. After the wine is made consumers can enjoy the aroma and flavor of the wine. Our gifts can be viewed in the same manner. There are assorted components of growth that we must go through to advance our gifts. Our very own gifts are going to require us to face our challenges and be uncomfortable. We must go through our own personal fermentation because this helps bring forth enlightenment. Enlightenment allows us to discover who we truly are and what we are destined to be. When we embody self-confidence and compassion, we can enjoy and share the gifts that we have discovered through God.

Ultimately, your journey requires you to be diligent in seeking God and grounding yourself in your daily spiritual practice. Be willing to learn, try, and understand that there will be some challenges. Having challenges does not mean that our life is not fair. It does not mean that we are not equipped to follow our dreams and embrace our creativity. No! Rather than getting trapped into a mindset of worry, you can trust that you are in a season of pruning and squeezing for elevation. Pruning involves a selective process for getting rid of things that no longer serve us for the greater good of our divine process. Squeezing requires us to undergo pressure that is uncomfortable, but later produces a grand experience to a purposeful life. We are meant to have a life that is filled with prosperity and oneness with God.

Notes

_____
_____
_____
_____
_____
_____
_____
_____
_____
_____
_____
_____
_____
_____
_____

Give Greatness
Gratitude Respect Encouragement Appreciation Time

Chapter 2
The GAP (Gratitude Awakening Practice)

Our oneness with God opens doors for the opportunity for personal growth. That is why it is necessary to rest at God's feet, spend time with God, and take time out of your day to just breathe, focusing on your daily breath, the pacing of your breath, and the beat of your heart. This is how you grow. Exhaling (breathing out) all of the worry and doubt and then Inhaling (breathing in) praise, compassion, and gratitude. Let Christ take the heavy load that is on your heart. You must take the load off yourself that family or society may place on you. With the many expectations and deadlines, we need a space to just be. To simply be in the Father's hands and to rest. When you are faithful to God with your practice of seeking God in meditation, prayer, and breathing, you will see a shift in your daily thought process, the words you speak, and your actions. You will go through a transformation but know that it is not enough to be motivated by the "Word" and promises of God. You are transformed by the renewal of your mind which means that you will begin to take action on the Word of God and apply it to your life daily. This is when you begin to seek God's will for your life and bring to light your purpose.

GAP Reflection Questions:

- What time in the morning are you willing to commit to setting aside to grow your Personal Relationship (PR) with God?

- What days of the week are you willing to devote to expanding your Personal Relationship (PR) time with God?

- How might you go about the process of holding yourself accountable?

- What personal experience has been most challenging for you?

- How did you feel when you were faced with this challenge?

- What steps have you taken to overcome this challenge?

GAP Reflection Exercise:

It is now time for you to take your spiritual practice a step further. You need to create a spiritual practice that is best for you to create a space for the Five Foundational Tools: **Practice, Meditation, Prayer, Self-Reflection, and Releasing**; therefore, allowing you to begin The Gratitude Awakening Practice or GAP. To discover your true self, it is essential for you to have a prayer closet.

I am talking about finding a secret place in your house where you close the door and get intimate with God. This space will allow you to grow even more in your Personal Relationship (PR) with God. You do not have to think hard about that space. My space, aka, my prayer closet, is my bathroom. In my bathroom, I have dedicated a wooden three-shelf that has specific items that help motivate, enhance and guide me to a more intentional spiritual practice and time with God. When creating this space remember that it is for You.

These items will help you to reach your highest potential of awareness and expression as you intentionally build a personal relationship with God:

- Bible and/or daily devotional book
- Journal/notepad and pen
- Picture of Family or Artwork
- Positive Quote or Affirmation
- Incense, Essential Oil Diffuser, or Candle

Matthew 6:6 (NIV)

"But when you pray, go into your room, close the door and pray to your Father, who is unseen. Then your Father, who sees what is done in secret, will reward you."

GAP Reflection Questions:

- Where is your prayer closet?

- Why did you select this space as your prayer closet?

- What are you wanting to gain from this experience?

Ecclesiastes 11:6-7 (NIV)
"Sow your seed in the morning, and at evening let not your hands be idle, for you do not know which will succeed, whether this or that, or whether both will do equally well. Light is sweet, and it pleases the eyes to see the sun."

Notes

Give Greatness
Gratitude Respect Encouragement Appreciation Time

The GAP Mindful Pace/Steps

Mindful Pace/Step (1)
Setting Up the Space

1. Find a place of solitude, a quiet place. I like my bathroom and I either have a candle, aromatherapy light, or incense. Depending on my mood.

2. Layout your prayer mat or prayer cloth. You can use a pillow to sit on, or a chair, or your couch. Again, this is a personal space that makes you feel the most comfortable and connected.

3. Have a glass of water in your space. It is important to stay hydrated and water reminds you of the importance of life.

Mindful Pace/Step (2)
Intentional Breathing

Before you start your daily spiritual practice of your Personal Relationship (PR) time with God. It is important that you find a space and or spot to sit and set your intention on your breathing. This can be in a chair, laying down on a mat, or sitting up. But the key aspect is to be comfortable.

Take a deep breath, inhale and exhale
 (say In the name of the Father)
Take another deep breath, inhale and exhale
 (say In the name of the Son)
Take another deep breath, inhale and exhale
 (say In the name of the Holy Spirit)

Then say: Gratitude.

This breathing pace is helping you set the intention for your spiritual practice and sends your heart, mind, body, and spirit the reminder of your purpose.

Mindful Pace/Step (3)
Daily Affirmation

As you read this book, I challenge you to say this affirmation every morning:

God's love never fails!
God's love and energy flow through me.
God is abundant and therefore I am open to receiving
an abundance of clarity, guidance, love, joy, peace, and prosperity.

Mindful Pace/Step (4)
Daily Prayer

Being intentional with prayer during your spiritual practice allows for you to connect with God on a personal level. Here is daily guidance on how to pray and remember that God is Great!

Give God **Gratitude**
Give God **Respect**
Let God give words to you of **Encouragement** (Remember what God did in the past and how far you have come).
Tell God you **Appreciate** Him
Give God **Time** to answer and come through with your prayers.
Amen.

Mindful Pace/Step (5)
Daily Journal of Self-Reflection

Take the time to write and self-reflect about your dreams, fears, and plans. These writings will help you navigate your thinking process and connect with yourself and other people around you.

Self-reflection is essential to personal growth. It also provides an avenue to direct your continued growth as an individual. In order to do this, you must follow the spirit and let go. Write what is in your heart and what is on your mind. We can't let what others believe or dictate what that may be.

Mindful Pace/Step (6)
Daily Reading
Set aside time to read the bible, a devotional, or a scripture-based text to provides more in-depth knowledge of who God is and what He said He would do in the word.
Reading the good word provides space for God to speak to you and to bring clarity into God's will for your life.

Mindful Pace/Step (7)
Daily Meditation
Take a deep breath. Slowly breathe in and out three times to clear your mind and focus on your breathing. Repeat this affirmation to yourself in your mind:

I am worth it!

Take another deep breath before repeating that affirmation in your mind several times. The more you say those words, you will start to see and feel a calmness in your breath, and your arms, shoulders, and jawline will become relaxed. You can use this guided practice and insert a different affirmation. Remember, the more you practice, the more you can ease your mind and breath.

Notes

Give Greatness
Gratitude Respect Encouragement Appreciation Time

Chapter 3
The ART
(Achieving Revolutionary Transformation) of Releasing Greatness

There are no such things as a challenge. It is simply an opportunity for growth and awareness. Yes, there are times when we feel like we are not enough, but when we truly begin to look within ourselves and reach out for help and guidance, God can provide us with the solution. It is important to see and understand the true meaning of giving without having a second thought and telling God that you are thankful for the opportunity to even give. God is amazing and wonderful, and we shouldn't doubt God's timing or ability to handle any situation. God is all-knowing, and He is great. By acknowledging and believing that God is great, He will continue to show out in your life in more than one way. There are miracles in our daily lives that we often take for granted. It is up to you to acknowledge and show gratitude for them. Therefore, using gratitude as an Energy-Shifting Tool raises your level of awareness of the true elevation of life and how much time we truly have here on Earth. The more miracles you can experience and appreciate, the more your life will enrich you, and you will celebrate more.

GAP Reflection Question:
What are some everyday miracles that occur in your life?

On Your Mark, Get Set and Reset!

Remember, you can always start now. You can start today by choosing to have a more profound experience in life. We should be striving towards greatness every single day. When you take time to truly do the inner work of self, you will begin to elevate your level of greatness and share it with the world. But first, your level of greatness must start with yourself and your family. That is when the true level of elevation, advancement, and ownership takes place.

The choices you make today have an impact on your tomorrow. You have to be mindful of your health, wealth, finances, and the company that you keep. So, with that being said, we have to be willing to give ourselves greatness and give greatness to others. It is imperative to practice self-reflection and release yesterday because today is a new day. You were born for greatness and it is time for you to walk in it.

Being great means giving **Gratitude, Respect, Encouragement, Appreciation,** and **Time** to yourself first and then to others. When you are intentional with your mind, body, emotions, goals, and commitment, it will help you navigate through a more purposeful and peaceful life.

Thank you, God, for making me great. I am full of Gratitude, Respect, Encouragement, Appreciation, and Time. Therefore, I will give Gratitude, Respect, Encouragement, Appreciation, and Time to others. Once I receive it in my heart, I know that I will be able to seize the day.

It is important that we are transparent with ourselves. We all face hardships and times of discouragement but let us be reminded that we will not be destroyed. We have greatness in us. We have the ability to overcome challenges at any time of our lives. We have the ability to transform our problems into a solution and flip it in a way to learn spiritually, physically, emotionally, or mentally, to enhance our earthly well-being. We all have a calling to help someone grow! We just have to be willing to examine our own areas of growth. Therefore, we are able to focus on ourselves and become better which requires us to know when it is time to reset.

Stepping back to reset is essential. Throughout my day, there are moments when I have to take a step back and reset. What I have realized throughout my life is the importance of my intentional practice that begins every day at 5:00 a.m. This is the time when I draw closer to God and discover more of my true self. It is beneficial to my spiritual needs and to my overall mental, emotional, and physical awareness to be the best version of myself. When it comes to motherhood, I have my moments when I am going from one task to the next and focused on busy work rather than intentionally taking time for myself. I am constantly on the go. We have gymnastics, swim class, basketball practice, and our weekly trips to the park. We are an outdoors family. Therefore, when I do not set aside my hour of being great and discovering my greatness I become stressed. I am thankful and grateful that I incorporate these practices into my life because it reminds me so much of how vital "Me time" is to me. My "Me time" is important for my family. My "Me time" is important for my community.

I decided to write this book because I want people all over the world to set aside "Me time" and be intentional about self-discovery and open up their true authentic selves. I want people across the entire planet to know that they have a voice and can do the unachievable and unimaginable. *Why?* Because everyone has a purpose and is able to move mountains and create masterpieces. All people are great, and it is up to you to dive deep into your greatness. Therefore, enjoy the gifts and tools God placed in you.

For you to enjoy the many gifts that you possess, you must walk in your divine way. Don't compare yourself to others. Comparing yourself to others does not bring a positive light to your mind, heart, and body. It can cause you to doubt the person that you have been designed to be. When we compare ourselves to others we are telling ourselves that we are not good enough, but in fact, we are! Your "Me time" is designed for you only and it allows you to understand that your journey is your journey. Be confident in your purpose and journey for your life! Embrace it. Learn from it. Then take a step towards greatness. Let's take the first step together. I believe when you step out on faith and trust God, you have to believe in yourself and know that God has you. You will then begin to activate your superpowers. Your superpowers are the armor of God.

Ephesians 6:10-18 (NIV)

"Finally, be strong in the Lord and in his mighty power. Put on the full armor of God, so that you can take your stand against the devil's schemes. For our struggle is not against flesh and blood, but against the rulers, against the authorities, against the powers of this dark world, and against the spiritual forces of evil in the heavenly realms. Therefore put on the full armor of God, so that when the day of evil comes, you may be able to stand your ground, and after you have done everything, to stand. Stand firm then, with the belt of truth buckled around your waist, with the breastplate of righteousness in place, and with your feet fitted with the readiness that comes from the gospel of peace. In addition to all this, take up the shield of faith, with which you can extinguish all the flaming arrows of the evil one. Take the helmet of salvation and the sword of the Spirit, which is the word of God. And pray in the Spirit on all occasions with all kinds of prayers and requests. With this in mind, be alert and always keep on praying for all the Lord's people."

Begin this season of elevation as the first step to acknowledging that there is a divine pathway to reaching your level of elevation and that you have the confidence to do it. Be aware that the map handed or given to you by society was not one-size-fits-all. You were not designed to conform or fit into the mold of others. You were designed to embrace the gifts and ideas that make you your authentic self. The more you are willing to take risks, be in the moment, and flow with life, life will produce more joy! Life has its way of providing a multitude of transformative energy and if you want to tap into this positive energy you must release the negative mindset of *What if...?* Your response should be *when this happens....* By being selective with the words that you speak, you discover that you hold the ultimate power to create greatness, but it's your choice to start the process. Choosing greatness is something you must constantly set aside and put in the work to grow inwardly. I believe when you do the inner work, your greatness will begin to flow outwardly. So, let's do the inner work to discover who we really are. Let's shed those layers and dig deep with the Five Fundamental Tools, **Practice, Meditation, Prayer, Self-Reflection,** and **Releasing**. When you apply your spiritual practice, you will be able to be great and give greatness to yourself and others through Energy Shifting Tools including **Gratitude, Respect, Encouragement, Appreciation,** and **Time.**

The "Shed Effect"

Understanding more of who God called you to be and what God ordained you to do is a divine experience. To discover your true self there are layers of uncertainties, doubts, fears, and insecurities that you must shed in order to draw closer to God and to discover your many gifts. I like to call this the "Shed Effect."

Shedding harmful thought patterns, beliefs, emotions, and uncertainties will allow you to go within to elevate your life. Life is all about growth. In the pursuance of growth, that means you have to make yourself accountable. Holding yourself accountable can be a struggle at times but remember that you do not want the same results. You should always be pushing towards elevation. If you are not willing to grow, then you are willing to remain stagnant. So, be willing to do the work to become a better you.

There are levels to the shedding experience that requires hard work, purposeful planning, practice, and patience to bring forth a stellar performance. Just like there are levels for a sprinter or runner to be able to experience a runner's high or be a professional runner for the Olympics. Each level requires a different game plan. Accountability requires you to switch and adjust create the mark and hit your goal. The same process applies to be a gymnast. There are various skills and levels that must be developed and mastered before you reach the level of Simone Biles, an American gymnast who has won over 30 Olympic gold medals and continues to strive towards greatness. The story of Simone is that she was not satisfied with winning one gold medal. No. She wanted to grow and elevate! She understood the sacrifices that she needed to make, including the long hours in the gym, maintaining a healthy and balanced diet, and making many other sacrifices. During her earlier years as a gymnast, she faced a lot of challenges, but she was determined to not be defeated. Simone Biles was willing to "Shed" in order to discover her greatness.

Think about someone you admire. Do you think those individuals gave up every time someone told them no, or when a door did not open at the time they wanted? No. They continued to let their compassion push them towards their dreams. They knew that God had called them to something greater than what their current circumstances were. I am a firm believer that when filled with compassion, God will allow you to experience peace when you are hit with storms, the world says, "No," or someone expects you to give up because what you're going through is hard. I am a firm believer that God will provide healing and will restore you when the world may say you are not strong enough. My friend, if we continue to allow what the world says, or others say, to determine our worth and our greatness, we are not living out what God has called us to do. Don't let anyone take your drive towards wanting to change for the better. When you are trying to follow your dreams, it requires change. I repeat, it requires you to change. Sometimes, that may mean that you are giving up things and people who you never thought you would, in order for you to win.

Release

Release is definitely a required practice and presents itself as an energy-shifting tool when implemented with consistency. As I reflect on releasing, I understand how powerful it is. Our minds are always in a constant state of moving and going into unknown territory that leads to various experiences. However, when we understand the beauty behind releasing, God can restore our mind, body, spirit, and heart. Releasing is something that you must be conscious of, knowing that it can help you in any situation that occurs.

When you release the many responsibilities, it can be refreshing to the mind, body, and spirit. Releasing is a powerful foundational tool and when you do release, healing, clarity, and patience are available to you. You will then be restored, rejuvenated, and renewed.

Restoration in your mind, body, heart, and spirit.
Rejuvenated in your mind, body, heart, and spirit.
Renewed in your mind, body, heart, and spirit.

Now imagine if you lived a life without releasing. I see it like you're in a huge thunderstorm in the middle of nowhere with no covering or shelter. Your body- head to feet- feels every cold droplet that touches your skin and clothes. Those cold droplets begin to sink into your skin leaving a colder feeling that is worse than the rain itself. You say that you have released the pain and the past hurt but when a storm comes, or uncertainty happens it's like the thunderstorm is still there. That means you haven't truly released that trauma, sin, or unpleasant experience. When you release, it brings forth relief. In an aim to truly release and start the healing process, you must release through **Practice, Meditation, Prayer, Self-Reflecting,** and **Releasing**. Holding on to pain-- trauma, sin, hurt, doubt, worry, fear, rejection, and insecurity-- can cause you to become stagnant in your Personal Relationship (PR) with God. When you wholeheartedly release your dreams, worries, and fears to God that is unique to you, God will provide you with clarity and peace. You are no longer wanting your will for your life, but you are wanting God's will for your life! Therefore, having a Personal Relationship (PR) requires you to seek God daily which provides rejuvenation and restoration.

There are reasons why we need to be restored. First, we are sinful, and we make mistakes. No one on earth is perfect. When we realize that we are not perfect and that we don't know it all, God will provide us with the ability to grow and remain humble. Second, even though we sin and make mistakes, I believe that we all have good intentions and are good people. However, at times, we do not make the best choices for ourselves and we have to clear our heart, mind, consciousness, and spirit to continue along the road to growth and elevation. You cannot be at your best if you are not willing to release.

When you are faithfully releasing your worries through prayer to God, it clears the pathway of weeds or clouds that would have hindered you from making a clear judgment on decisions in your daily life. Having a sound and clear judgment allows you to be able to hear and see the direction God wants you to go. By releasing those prayers to God, He then is able to share His grace and mercy.

Hebrews 4:16 (NIV)
"Let us then approach the throne of grace with confidence, so that we may receive mercy and find grace to help us in our time of need."

The beautiful aspect of The GAP is that it is a divine translation between you and God. This road travelled does not require anything from anyone else. God has designed a road map that has been created for you only! This is your personal journey and it's a purpose for you and God. When you have a PR, you are allowing the Holy Spirit to guide you with decision-making and provide opportunities for growth. It opens a doorway for you to activate compassion towards yourself and your journey. It is only when we connect compassion towards release, then we can reconnect back to our true self and discover more of what we haven't yet unlocked on this journey called life. In my first book

The Power of Change: Understanding Your Resilience In the Midst of Growth I discuss the importance of having a PR and how it can help you communicate with God. Now, let's get ready to unlock your greatness!

Unlocking Your GREAT Box

Take a second to think about your mind as a box. You have the ability to open or close your mind, heart, body, and spirit to new concepts and practices. You also have the knowledge to expand. A box has a lid and when you put the lid over your thinking, concepts, and practices you are not able to flow. It is imperative to your individual journey that you have a growth mindset and are willing to learn from others and not stay stagnant.

"In a growth mindset, people believe that their most basic abilities can be developed through dedication and hard work... brains and talent are just the starting point. This view creates a love of learning and a resilience that is essential for great accomplishment" (Dweck, 2015).

When you want to change and believe that you have the capacity to change, that will create a spark. This spark will create enlightenment of various sensations in your mind to generate change. You will then begin to do research and put into practice the mindset that you want to grow in your greatness. During this time, you will start to have some wins. You will also notice that you are moving into a more mindful and positive space. You are dedicating yourself to a growth mindset and to become an exceptional person. Your mind is dimensional, and it is imperative that you discover the various thought patterns, experiences, and abilities that you have to become your highest self. When you open your mind, you gain more insight and know-how to navigate from worldly distractions.

The more you slide the lid to the side or take your lid off, the more **Gratitude, Respect, Encouragement, Appreciation,** and **Time** you can give yourself and others. Don't be in a rush to take the whole lid off at one time. It is truly a process. Take your time. You want to acknowledge the miracles, the knowledge, and the energy to flow and be consistent and present. You want this foundational practice to cling with you. You want to create a sense of awareness in yourself that provides you with divine confidence and clarity.

Having an awareness is key to an essential practice as well as knowing the importance to tap in more with your true self. The distractions of the world can make you have moments of unclarity and uncertainty. You must be able and willing to practice the art of releasing and self-reflection. When you release what you have been holding onto, it allows you to receive strength and confidence from God, therefore, cultivating a worry-free life. The foundational tool of releasing is a refining moment of mental growth that tends to ground self-reflection. Another foundational tool is self-reflection and it is a key component of growth to better understand your true self. This practice causes you to think twice about your life and how to have gratitude towards yourself and others.

The more you tune in with the flow of your life, the more you are able to express your true self and witness even bountiful blessings. Being in the flow is the pure immersion of tranquillity, enjoyment, and harmony of an occurrence. Many times, being in the flow causes us to lose track of time. This is when you begin to realize that this moment is a divine connection that leads to a miraculous transaction. There are everyday miracles and we should be open to receiving them. Life is about adventures of joy, love, peace, and prosperity. Too often, we are not taking a look at the blessings of nature and life around us. Having an awareness allows us to see the creative designs of God's handy work.

Constantly we are distracted by our phones, social media, shopping, friends, and work. This can stop us from discovering our true selves. Meaning it stops our flow of energy of becoming our greatest self and discovering more of who God has called us to be. While it is a good thing to spend time with family, friends and go on those fun outings, you have to find quiet time for yourself, as an individual, to rebuild, refocus, and reground before you start your day. That is why releasing is so profound.

Set the Space and Pace

Your story, your thoughts, and your experiences are divine and unique. Your ability to self-reflect is a true and definitive key to unlocking your inner growth and light to share with others. I heard one time from one of my favorite movies, *Eat Love Pray*, "You have to be selective with your thoughts just like you are selective with your clothing." Your mind is powerful and is capable of generating phenomenal designs of creativity. I believe, once you tap into your God-given gifts that He has blessed you with, you will have the prominent information to write down the clear purpose for your life. The more you are intentional with yourself and God, the more you can dig deep to explore various roots of your life. We are human and we all have experienced moments of joy, pain, loss, and sorrow. However, despite the emotional journey that we are on, it is critical to creating a space to write and release these experiences. One way to release is through journaling. Journaling allows us to name the experience and emotion. It gives us the space and opportunity to push towards a path of renewal and rejuvenation of moving to a higher version of self. When we strip off various layers of past emotions and experiences, we are then able to tap into our highest self. Our society places so much emphasis on following the trends, making financial gains, and the pursuit of happiness by material means, but does not provide space and opportunity for you to STOP and release. These are all distractions that can stop you from living out your life's purpose and achieving your goals.

I say yes, move towards your dreams and push towards elevation! While you strive for greatness, always push to be your best self. The more time you are intentional with yourself and learning how to peel back those layers of your inner struggles, whether they are insecurity, hurt, pain, loss, and fear, the more you can discover new gifts and talents that you never thought you had. I want you to take hold of the unique vision that God has designed for you. Understand that God has already placed everything you need. Don't get distracted, you must continue to stay the course and focus on your personal growth and what you can control. Sometimes we believe that we need people to know everything about us with 24/7 access. We are constantly checking our phones, emails, social media, calls, and texting others. We have limitless apps to make our lives more convenient but think of all the shared access you have given others unwillingly and how it can cause a strain or disconnect from the source (God) and your family. God wants us to access Him anytime and to know that we have the ability to do that. God is with us and when we take that initial step to **Practice Prayer, Meditation, Self-Reflection,** and **Releasing**, you can access God anytime you want.

Best and believe that when you embark on this journey, it will be the most powerful avenue of transfer of energy. This transformational energy is what you want and need. This energy and newfound perspective of growth are indescribable. This transformational energy is something that no one can take away. The greatness about God is that you can access God here and now! No fret, the expansion of knowledge is available for you and in order to achieve it, you must first be willing to put in the work. It won't happen overnight, but eventually, you discover that your knowledge and foundational base are increasing. Therefore, you are able to utilize the information to help spread love and light to others.

Believing is receiving and receiving is believing. So, be willing to believe and receive knowledge and know that it can re-open a new world of emotional, physical, mental, and spiritual transactions that you have possessed since you entered this world.

Self-Reflection

Have you ever looked in the mirror and asked yourself, "Is this really me?" "I love what I see!" "I love who I am." Not just the physical appearance, but my emotional, spiritual and mental." In order to truly love yourself and understand the power of change, you must be ready and willing to self-reflect. Self-Reflection is a powerful process that can impact your outlook on life for the better when implemented daily. Self-Reflection enhances your ability to be fully aware of your inner thoughts and the processes you make to get there. This process is a whole new level of awareness that some are not able to fully grasp until they have reached recognition. I believe there are levels to achieving self-reflection.

During this process, you will elevate your mind to the highest concept of self and you will consciously recognize your true self in its most rewarding state.

Self-Reflection requires you to transform your thinking to new levels of consciousness. You will become more aware of your thoughts, feelings, and environment. Therefore, optimizing your ability to seek your highest self of ultimate performance. Not striving toward perfection but for progress and understanding. You have to understand that living intentionally is an everyday process. Four elements are designed to bring forth awareness allowing one to fully self-reflect. These elements include your mind, heart, body, and spirit.

GAP Reflection Exercise:

Find a space that you can have complete solitude to complete these guided self-reflection questions. Be willing to set aside 20 minutes to complete this activity on a separate sheet of paper.

GAP Reflection Questions:

1. *Use your mind*
    a. *What do you think about yourself?*

2. *Use your ears*
    a. *What do you hear from your inner self?*
    b. *If what you hear is positive... congratulate yourself and celebrate.*
    c. *If what you hear is negative... address it as an area of growth.*
    d. *Pause and give it 1 minute and respond to self in a way that gives encouragement showing yourself self-grace to learn and make mistakes*

  e. Whether what you hear is positive or negative, always end it with a positive

3. Use your mouth
  a. What do you speak/say to your inner self?
  b. Speak positivity to yourself.
  c. Have an affirmation or two to help you remember your why.
  d. It is important to understand the narrative that your mind plays. However, it is more dynamic to address the narrative that provides clarity and authenticity to self-reflection.

4. Use your spirit/heart
  a. What do you feel?
  b. What do you hear?
  c. Say motivating scriptures or affirmations to help guide you towards strength.

After this self-reflection process, you should feel relief and acknowledgment of gratitude towards yourself, due to taking the time to self-reflect. Tell yourself "Thank you" for taking time for yourself. Another self-reflection practice can be incorporated in the morning or the evening before bed. This requires only 5-10 minutes of your time and helps you to start the process of being more intentional and aware of the daily blessings that occur in your life. Before I close my eyes, this guided daily and weekly self-reflection practice helps me keep myself centered.

Notes

Give Greatness
Gratitude Respect Encouragement Appreciation Time

Monday (Gratitude)	Write ways in which you showed **Gratitude** or how it was given to you.
Tuesday (Respect)	Write ways in which you showed **Respect** or how it was given to you.
Wednesday (Encouragement)	Write ways in which you showed **Encouragement** or how it was given to you.
Thursday (Appreciation)	Write ways in which you showed **Appreciation** or how it was given to you.
Friday (Time)	Write ways in which you showed **Time** or how it was given to you.
Saturday & Sunday (Free Choice)	You can write how you have given greatness to yourself and others.

Self-Reflection Guided Practice: Nightly

Respect

Learning to be gentle with yourself may be a difficult concept to grasp and put into practice. Thinking about this concept as a mother reminds me of the times I have had to be gentle with my kids and the ones I love. But how am I supposed to show and be gentle with myself? Respect starts with you being great towards yourself. Showing respect towards oneself is very important and essential for your growth. If you don't love and honor yourself and aren't gentle with yourself, you will not unlock the authentic purpose for your life. When you refuse to unlock your greatness, you are creating a blockage that clogs your core. Your core is connected to your highest self. The core is the most important part of yourself and when it is not clogged it can open a world of enlightenment and awakening that you have never seen or felt.

Before we entered the world, we were granted a divine purpose with extraordinary gifts. However, somewhere in life, we got lost, disconnected, or rerouted from our authentic self and connection to nature. We may have become distracted due to societal pressures or sin which causes an interruption or pause in the flow of energy called life that is in our core. We begin to make choices that are not suitable for our growth. Does it hinder us from receiving ultimate peace with who we are called to be? So, now as adults, we seek a deep source of connection that allows us to just be and have joy. I have to be real with you. The connection that you long for is already inside of you. God lives in each and every one of us. We just have to stay connected. The more time you invest in yourself and spiritual practice, the more you will discover your authentic self and what God has for you. When you respect yourself, you are willing to appreciate, acknowledge and encourage others to see their greatness. Yes, showing greatness does require energy and time. But, I believe the more we are great with ourselves by discovering our authentic self, the more we can show greatness to others and change the world. This is the act of showing greatness. For you to reach this level of greatness, it will require you to be open to receiving new knowledge.

We all know that reading is fundamental. However, it is only fundamental when you apply the new knowledge you've acquired to your life. Every form of a word, book, translated Bible, self-discovery, health-conscious, and other books can be used to grow your personal relationship with Christ and into the discovery of your highest self. In order to grow and discover more about life, you must be willing to read the word of God daily and listen to your heart to determine how the word can be applied to your life. When you begin to meditate on the word of God you can see a lesson to be taught or learned.

The Bible or good Word has sound instruction and guidance that can provide you with the reading practice used to strengthen your faith, inner core, spirit, and mind. It is not just enough to read the Bible. You have to also be willing to look within yourself to discover in what ways God is speaking to you. When you apply your reading to life it creates a firm application, that is when you know reading is truly fundamental. Reading the Bible during your PR time guides you as you journey through your greater purpose.

GAP Reflection Exercise:

Read Jeremiah 29: 11-13 (NIV). After reading the verses, write down five to six words that resonate with you. In what ways has God shown up in your life?

Jeremiah 29:11-13 (NIV)
"For I know the plans I have for you," declares the Lord, "plans to prosper you and not to harm you, plans to give you hope and a future. Then you will call on me and come and pray to me, and I will listen to you. You will seek me and find me when you seek me with all your heart."

After reading these verses, it reminded me that God always keeps his promises and how sometimes we can be forgetful of how God has delivered us from past heartache. No matter the circumstances, we should be thankful for the time we have and be intentional with our time, knowing that God is with us. You will enhance your life by intentionally spending time with God to build a personal relationship with Him.

The GAP or Gratitude Awakening Practice requires a daily process of **Practice, Prayer, Meditation, Self-Reflection,** and **Releasing**. This practice will allow you to show greatness through gratitude, respect, encouragement, appreciation, and time to yourself and others. When we are able to do this, we are able to see a positive shift in our interactions, conversations, responses, and overall perspectives. As I always say: You can only control what you can control. Be willing to realize the power you have and step out on faith. The power of change comes when you are willing to step out on faith and understand that you are resilient in the midst of growth.

The power of your words can help shift your energy and perspective. Words of affirmation help start the process of claiming strength and give you motivation. Have you ever heard of speaking what you want, need, or desire into existence? When you speak affirmations aloud, you are releasing words that are positive from your heart and spirit into the universe. When you speak words of motivation and align your words with an action plan and purpose, the more you will discover your true self. It's only when you have a clear practice and utilization of God's word, that you are able to grow strong in the purpose that God has designed for your life.

GAP Reflection Questions:

- *Think of a time when you did not show respect to yourself.*
  - *How could you have given respect to yourself?*
  - *What "word" or "phrase" can you say to remind yourself that you deserve respect?*

Prayer. The power of prayer! When you set aside time with God and you are intentional with your prayer life, God hears and knows your heart. Consistency is the key when praying with practice. Whenever you hear a calming sound in your ear, a nudge, or tug on your heart, follow the spirit. That is your spirit calling upon you to guide you to come closer to God. Don't let distractions detach you from the truth and the journey and purpose God has placed inside of you. Before you were even born, God knew what you would be, and He placed greatness in you. But, how often do we set aside time to really tap into that greatness and utilize it to change ourselves, our family, and the world? Our inner gifts and talents that are inside of us should not be covered or disregarded. It should be shared to lift someone up and to change the world. So often, we wonder why we haven't obtained a level of understanding, a guilt-free life, and a life of prosperity. It is because we keep allowing ourselves to fall deeper into what society wants us to be instead of what God wants us to be. That is why it is so essential to read, pray, and practice. You must establish a routine that embodies **Practice, Prayer, Meditation, Self-Reflection,** and **Release**.

That is how one gains insight into the true beauty and nature of your true self by being intentional with your spiritual practice. This journey called life can be somewhat challenging at times and can cause you to think that you do not have the tools to succeed, but I am here to tell you that you can and will. You must find the inner strength and grit to do the things that aren't ordinary to the majority of people. That means taking bold leaps of faith and staying consistent even when you feel like giving up. When you commit to practicing consistency in prayer, that is when you will get an extraordinary response and produce change. Sometimes you must be willing to change the application to get better results.

Prayer is essential. Prayer is an indispensable tool that can and will change your life and daily perspective. Prayer, when rooted in your spirit and heart, will help you stay in alignment with God and your highest self. When you pray with purpose, the more you will feel rooted and connected to your foundation and the spirit.

Prayer is a powerful practice. Sometimes I question myself asking, "How do I even start?" But then, I realize that I am in my head and emotions. Even worse, I start to judge myself and the process. I begin to take a few deep breaths and realize that no matter what words I say, what emotions flow, or thoughts that may surface that God knows my heart and God will answer my prayers. When I am in prayer, I ask God for strength, covering, clarity, reflection, and perseverance. I am a firm believer that when you sincerely seek God with all your heart that there will be a shift in your spirit and a stride in your step towards your purpose of fulfillment.

Prayer is a beautiful practice. Prayer presents a sacred space, time, and opportunity for you and God to connect on a personal level. When done with a clear heart and intentions, God is able to guide you.

Let the words of my mouth be acceptable and pleasing to you.

Often, there are times when I don't know what I am going to pray for, but when I start my prayer off with the moment of gratitude my heart, spirit, and mind do the rest. The more you pray the more connected you are with God and self. The more you are able to stand against the odds of the world and have peace in your life. I believe that prayer does change things. However, it is up to us to also take initiative and do the work in the prayer. For example, if you are asking God to provide you with a job or a healthy lifestyle. You must be willing to take action. You must put in the application. Prayer without works or action will not get you closer to receiving the blessing behind the prayer.

Prayer is helpful. Prayer renews your mind, as well as setting your attention and intention for the day! It helps you to refocus, regroup, and understand the faith walk that you are on. It also reminds you of the importance of taking the time to acknowledge others who need support or help. Pray to withstand all that life brings in all areas of your life, including health, mind, body, spirit, family, finances, relationships, and career. Prayers come from the heart and are heard and received. When you pray, believe in the words that you are saying. Let them remind you that you must continue to press and push through whatever you may be facing.

Prayer is releasing. Prayer allows you to release words of meaning to God and help you to discover your true self. Prayer takes many different forms. It doesn't matter when or how you pray. It doesn't matter if it is long or short. As long as you pray, that is all that matters. Be intentional with your prayer time with God. Through prayer, you can reclaim, re-establish, and reconnect with the promises of God. Again, words are meaningful and powerful. Words have the power to uplift, connect yourself to God, and uphold the purpose of your life.

The Dynamic Duo of Gratitude and Appreciation. Having gratitude and appreciation is another form of practice that you must incorporate into your prayer life. Giving thanks for your past, present, and future. This allows you to see the true beauty of life and how everything you do has meaning and purpose. It allows for you to self-reflect on yesterday, the day before, and for you to take hold and advantage of the current day. When you are able to stop, breathe, and self-reflect during your daily morning practice, you are showing appreciation. This practice reminds you of the importance of listening within and trusting your growth process. You must first acknowledge that all growth, goals, and gathering of information for gaining and sustaining knowledge must be first acknowledged with self and then put into practice. Through this practice, you will experience wins and gain strength.

Gratitude is essential to realize the true energy of love and light that is already inside of you. You have the divine gift of spreading it. It is important to recognize and display gratitude to those who inspire your life on a daily basis. Gratitude is what makes the love flow from one heart to another heart. It is the unspoken language at times from one kindred spirit to the next. For example, saying to someone, "I see you, and I am grateful for you," is a way to show gratitude. Intentionally appreciating someone can bring positive energy, peace, and clarity to a person's soul. All people want love, acknowledgment, and to belong.

Practicing gratitude allows you to show and tell others how much you are grateful for who they are or an action that they made. Taking the time to appreciate others brings joy to yourself and allows you to receive something in a greater return. Isn't that what life is all about? Being able to take time and express appreciation, gratitude, and lift others. This spiritual practice will remind you of the importance of staying connected to God as the source. God is the light within you that will travel and enlighten you to your calling and will guide you to yourself. Stay connected with God. There is power in having gratitude. When you release gratitude, you are opening opportunities for greatness, appreciation, and joy to flow through yourself and others. The Energy Shifting Tool of gratitude sends positive energy into your heart, mind, body, and spirit.

Therefore, a meaningful feeling and experience are created and stored in your memory bank. The more gratitude we display and give helps us understand more about ourselves to elevate our thinking. The more you practice, the more aware you are of things that you may take for granted. Plus, your stress load will decrease because you are not focusing on people, what they have, or who they are. You are too busy being thankful and showing gratitude towards yourself. Gratitude allows you to have the right perspective. Please, keep it dear to your heart.

Life is a beautiful journey. The ability to see, hear touch, and feel is a blessing that I know we may take for granted. Throughout my life, I have discovered that there cannot be a balance when you are not self-reflecting and not being mindful of the daily choices that you make. It is imperative that you recognize that your emotions are connected to the choices that you make. When you are dedicated to your personal growth, there must be a balance with giving time to self, family, and God. Authentic balance is always flowing and never stagnant. This means you are faith-walking in your purpose and trusting God to guide you in the directions you need to take. Yes, there will be moments when you are not balanced and that is okay. Recognize where that emotion is coming from, then address the emotion and move on. Despite the emotions you may have, the journey continues. Take moments to honor and respect yourself for who you are and what you bring to this journey. If you do not respect and appreciate yourself for who you are, then how can you expect others to do the same? It starts with self. It is okay to create boundaries, so you can embody your greatness.

GAP Reflection Exercise:

- *What does it look, sound, and feel like when you are unbalanced?*

- *What are some things you can do to get you re-centered when you are unbalanced?*

- *How can you create boundaries, so you can be your best self?*

When you are trying to elevate your life in **Practice, Meditation, Prayer, Self-Reflection,** and **Releasing**, you will experience various challenges. *Why?* You are pushing your mind, body, and spirit into a new place, and you are strengthening muscles that you did not expect and know existed. So, I tell you this, when faced with a challenge, keep pushing. That challenge is an opportunity to grow and become more resilient. Take the time to appreciate who you are and are destined to be. Don't get stuck on the negative. Don't get stuck in the last season. Don't get stuck in the challenge. Sometimes we limit ourselves in various beliefs, which holds us back from success. Don't let negativity, whether it is people or situations, hold you back from your present! Step out on faith and push towards your goals. You must release and break focus on what you have going on now! The mind is powerful and when we release negative thoughts, emotions, and experiences to God that we are facing, we are trusting that our prayers will be answered! We just have to trust and know that what we prayed about has already been taken care of. We have to show that God has answered our prayers through our actions.

Meditation. According to the Merriam-Webster Dictionary, Meditation is having the ability to engage in mental exercise (such as concentration on one's breathing or repetition of a mantra) for the purpose of reaching a heightened level of spiritual awareness. Meditation truly is a powerful experience. Having this spiritual awareness allows for you to create space between yourself and this world. When you take time to create space and opportunity for meditation you are able to have a deeper connection with how your mind, body, spirit, and soul are all connected. However, the spiritual process of meditation requires you to go deep into the core (heart) of your spirit. Meditation does take time and it is essential to your GAP. Here are five elements for meditation:

- ★ *Meditation is personal*
- ★ *Meditation is patience*
- ★ *Meditation is peaceful*

- ★ *Meditation is priceless*
- ★ *Meditation is pure*

Let's take a look at how these five elements can be utilized to enhance your spiritual practice.

Meditation is personal. Meditation allows for you to take the time to go deep within your core to explore the stillness and an abundant ability to seek peace within. Meditation requires you to focus on your breath and mind. You have to give yourself grace with meditation.

Meditation is patience. Mediation is a personal art and there is no improper way to meditate. Why? Because it is personal. You have to be willing to understand that this is a personal practice that requires patience from you. There will be times that you will go in and out of meditation (that is completely normal) however, you must start back again and keep pushing. Always giving yourself grace.

Meditation is peaceful. Be intentional with the space that you are in when you are deciding to set aside "Me time" when you are wanting to meditate. You want to make sure that it is quiet. If it is not quiet, then use music (I personally love the calming ocean and tribal sounds) to help set the space. When you incorporate this into your breathing or mantras it can enhance your meditation practice.

Meditation is priceless. You cannot put a value or price on meditation. Meditation at times can be hard to explain because it is personal. Everyone's journey is unique to their purpose, therefore, everyone's experience while meditation may not be the same. However, millions of people understand how powerful this Energy Shifting Tool can enhance their well-being.

Meditation is pure. While meditating you must give yourself grace, knowing that in the midst of meditation that it is a judgment-free zone. No wrong can occur in the process. That is why meditation is pure because it produces such a sweet and delicate warmth at your core.

Meditation really is a practice and the more you practice the more you are in tune with yourself. When you are in tune with yourself the more you are in tune with your thoughts, therefore allowing you to flow into becoming more aware and sympathetic towards others. In this world, everyone is going through something and trying to find their way through. The more you honor life-- nature, family, and community-- you will allow for your greatness to spread and will inspire others too. This mere act will allow you to "find" your way through.
By embedding meditation as a foundational tool, it can be a prominent step into deepening the level of your inner greatness. The more you release and practice, the more you can strengthen your mind. But also, your core (heart) and spirit. All forms of your "Me time" self-care journey require you to be mindful and to have a mindset shift during your growth of acceleration and elevation. In order to do so, meditation is the start of that. Meditation requires you to stop, breathe and focus on one thing which could be a mantra, recurring sound, picture, or word. Let us make a creed to meditate and become our highest self. You have it in you to have more compassion and empathy towards serving others. You have the gift to spread love and light. When you are still, you can hear God, connect with your higher self, hear your thoughts, and seize the possibilities of the day. I will be honest with you that there is no one way or step to follow meditation. However, there are several meditation apps and readings online. Use the web to increase your knowledge. That is always a great first stop. Remember meditation comes within and there is no wrong way to meditate. It is what works best for you!

GAP Reflection Exercise:

Here are some recommendations on how to start meditation. I suggest starting with one minute and then gradually increase your time to five minutes. Before the end of the day, find a quiet spot, focus on your breath and give it a try. After meditating, write down how you felt during the practice. The more you practice, the more it will flow. Remember it is a process. Always feel free to refer back to Mindful/Pace (Step 6) Meditation for guidance.

Rest to Reset. It is a beautiful pleasure to rest in the arms of the Father knowing and understanding that God provides us with peace, clarity, and guidance. Rest is a form of releasing. Rest gives your body a chance to rejuvenate itself from daily routines and responsibilities. Rest is essential to your daily practice of releasing. When you truly release, you are handing your worries, doubts, fears, and dreams over to God. You are saying, "I trust you to do and bring forth the promises and words that you have given and declared to me since the beginning of time." When you are communicating to God that you only want what is best to you and the purpose that has been shared with you; you do not have time to be involved in other people's business. The only business that should concern you is the purpose that is for you.

I know it can be a challenging concept for some to do. Why? Because we like to be in control of everything and everyone else. Some of us enjoy being *nositrians*, meaning we know what is going on with everyone else, but neglect what is going on in our lives. We should only be concerned with what impacts our lives and how we can better ourselves. True wisdom is knowing that there are notions of things that we must leave for God and the truth of the matter is we shouldn't want to know it all. This is especially true when it comes to our life. It then takes out the surprise factor, and we are unable to enjoy the process of growing into the holistic human that God called and aligned us to be. So, release and be set free. Rest is necessary for the development of your greatness.

Another powerful practice is the ability to understand when to pause and release. Our society often tells us that we need to go, go, go and we will sleep when we are dead. But, it is critical for you to be intentional about the time that you rest. Resting is a form of releasing. Being able to release for just a short 20-minute nap is a way for you to recharge and refocus for the day. Maybe you are not a napper. Okay, maybe you can find a quiet space or put on music for 10-15 minutes to do a quick breathing or meditation practice. Maybe you are a stretcher or all of the above. What I am saying is that it is important that you take time to release stress. Understand that your body, mind, and heart will thank you for taking the time to release. Release, Let Go, and Let God. When you do this practice, you can Release, Refocus, and Reset.

Oftentimes, people say that rest is not important, but there is power in being still and resting. Sometimes people only get three to four hours of rest, when it's important to get seven to nine hours of sleep. I realized how important it is for me to have a day of rest and be still. I decided that Monday-Saturday would be my 5 a.m. morning. During the week, I follow a routine that is structured so I can exercise, write, pray and grow. By waking up early it allows me to grow and be my best version of myself. I am also able to have more energy, not be stressed, and have less stress. Believe me, the foods we eat and the liquids we drink play a critical role in our emotions and overall health.

GAP Reflection Question:
What are some activities you do to rest?

Water is an essential element and requirement to function as a human being. Our bodies are made of 80 percent water, but, as humans, we still do not drink enough of it. It is a way to cleanse, detox, and refresh and replenish our bodies. Water provides nutrients for the body, mind, heart, and spirit. When you drink water, it is able to flow to every part of your body and replace the missing nutrients that are missing. There are many health benefits to drinking water.

According to *Healthline*, there are seven scientific benefits to drinking water.

1. *Helps Maximize Physical Performance*
2. *Significantly affects energy levels and brain function*
3. *May help and prevent headaches*
4. *May help relieve constipation*
5. *May help treat kidney stones*
6. *Helps prevent hangovers*
7. *Can aid weight loss*

So, challenge yourself while you are reading this book to start drinking more water. If you currently drink three glasses of water let's increase it to five glasses of water. Before you know it you will be drinking the recommended amount of water that you need for your body. Here is an idea. Before you start your daily spiritual practice of Personal Relationship (PR) time, have a bottle or glass of water nearby. Drink water when you first get up out of your bed. Drink the water while you are in The GAP with **Practice, Prayer, Meditation, Self-reflecting,** and **Releasing**. Before you know it, you will have completed your first glass of water and the Five Essential Tools. I personally place a bottle of water on my nightstand every night and as soon as my alarm goes off at 5:00 a.m. (Monday-Saturday), I immediately give thanks to God above, put on my house shoes, and start drinking.

GAP Reflection Exercise:

- How many glasses of water do you drink in a day?

- What do you do in the last hour before you rest or get ready for bed?

- Do you take time to reflect on the day? If so, what do you do?

- Begin journaling for 10 minutes reflecting on the positive moments of the day.

Time. Time is valuable and often we say we don't have enough time in the day to get things done, go after our dreams, or set a goal. Well, I have news for you regardless of your position, title, sex, wages, or weight. You have time. It is all about setting your intention and understanding the need to make the best of the time you do have to set goals. Push and work towards those goals to become wins. Then, those wins will become your dream. You can do it! Start now, start planning, and mapping out what you can do.

No matter how busy you are and how you start your day, it is important that you are intentional about setting aside time for personal growth and development. There will be times where your routine, time, or obligations may change but you must continue to push and grow knowing that the time you spend on the mat or prayer cloth is essential to your well-being, mentally, physically, emotionally, and spiritually. It is a great opportunity for you to dial in and see the day ahead.

True alignment occurs when you are intentional with time. Have you ever heard of the saying: time is of the essence? When you are intentional with the time, you are able to be more giving, loving, and useful to accomplish the goals you have set forth for the day. You will understand the importance of family, work, and goals. There is enough time to make gains and to give back. Time is about gains and giving. When you give of your time and it is something you want, you will gain personal and spiritual blessings within it. There will be an awakening of energy of gratitude, respect, encouragement, appreciation, and time. Acknowledging that the time you have decided to share and give to that person is a gift and should be honored.

Practice. Practice, practice, practice makes perfect. That is what we all heard as children, right? But I believe that when you practice, practice, practice, it creates lasting results. When you are intentional with the time that you spend with God in that "Me Time" and "Prayer Closet Time," and you stick with it, your life will change. You are showing dedication, commitment, perseverance, and diligence to God and yourself. You are showing up each and every time because you want to grow in your relationship with Christ and you want God to help guide you into elevation and maintain a heart of gratitude. Practice is when you are putting your mind, heart, and spirit into training. God has to coach you for expansion, therefore, producing growth and alignment with your purpose. If God showed and told you all that would occur in your life, your mind would not be able to receive or even conceive it. So, it is important that you enjoy this journey called life and embrace the unknown. Open your mind to practice growth in order to train and change for the better. Again, align yourself with God to discover your true self.

Each and every day you have breath, it is a miracle. Being able to take a step on the pavement is a miracle. Every movement in your body that you make is a gift from God. It is a reminder to give thanks and to show gratitude to God. Taking intentional breaths is freeing and creates a flow of a practice that is peaceful. Your breaths help control your mind, heart, and body. It also helps with self-control. Breathing allows for you to realign and re-center with God. When you first wake up and your alarm goes off. Don't be so quick to jump out of the bed. Take a few moments to take deep breaths in and out. Focusing on the peace of the day. Give thanks to God for waking you up this morning. You should just flow. Get in the practice of doing this daily. Breathing is a form of energy. Energy is connected to life and God. When you are structuring your breath with breathing exercises you are able to connect with and tap into your heart, mind, body, soul, and emotions.

Release for forgiveness. When we think of forgiveness, we often think it is for the other person. The same thing goes for apologies and saying I'm sorry. Forgiveness is the change for renewal of the heart, mind, body, and spirit. But when forgiveness occurs, it must start with the heart and mind. Oftentimes when we say we forgive the person, we still hold on to the psychological and heart component of the very thing the person did. For you to truly grow and release, you must release it from all areas. Of course, this depends on what the person did because your heart, mind, body, and spirit may need time. It is about you releasing yourself from the energy, hurt, or pain that the person has or had caused and that will start the healing journey for you. The powerful thing behind forgiveness is that the person who caused pain doesn't even have to apologize. Yes, it helps many of us feel better to hear those words, but it should not be co-dependent or dependent solely on the words of that person. We should not look for healing from that person.

You have to go inward for you to heal instead of going outward and looking for quick satisfaction including purchases, likes on social media, or love from a person that is not good for us. Look, we have all been down that road before, so it is up to us, "me", the power of you to forgive that person and release yourself from that "thing." Start discovering your true self and understand more of what and who God has called you to be. Stop with the excuses and start with the healing. Maybe counseling or therapy is a healthy option. Maybe you need a trusted spiritual advisor. Maybe you need to seek a life coach. The main point is to start the process, so you can be there for the ones you love. I know you can be there for your family in ways that they need you and to give back to your community. Believe me, a person is out there waiting for you to uplift and spread and command greatness.

Gratitude, gratitude, and then more gratitude. This word is so simple but so profound. Having gratitude towards God is a symbolic experience. You can practice having gratitude throughout your day. There are so many sweet moments throughout the day to release gratitude. You can release gratitude throughout your day starting in the morning with your Personal Relationship (PR) time with God, family, and during the enjoyment of food, time, touch, sounds, a profound thought of the day, and moments of peace and clarity. Ask God to give you an awakening to start noticing the moments of gratitude expressed and given on a daily basis.

Notes

Give Greatness
Gratitude Respect Encouragement Appreciation Time

Closing

Throughout your life's journey, there will be times when you are not at your best. Maybe, you feel down, or you are figuring out your emotions. Well, I have a moment of transparency. I often have similar days when I don't always feel at my best when my mind and heart are sometimes heavy. However, I still push through by taking mini-breaks to pray and deep breaths to meditate to re-center myself. During these times, I have realized that when you are trying something new, you will be tested. This is especially true when you are taking time to grow in your personal life and connect with your higher self. That is all a part of the process.

I have realized that everything that I ever wanted to do and have, I had to work hard for. Nothing was given to me and I must continue to push throughout the whole process. I must continue to show greatness to myself and understand that God created me and designed me for greatness. That there is only one me and that's what makes the story unique. The trauma and societal pressures did have me worried and insecure at first, but not anymore. I will continue to spread my wings. I also know and understand that comparison is dangerous and that you should only want the arenas and places that God wants you to go and do. There is a lane for everyone and it is up to me to give greatness to others, but also give greatness towards myself. It is important for me to be confident in who I am and who God has called me to be and do. It is important for me to love more of myself. I see and receive more of myself. I appreciate and trust the process of my journey.

In the process of writing this book, I discovered the true power of having a spiritual practice that leads to sustaining the foundational and energy-shifting tools that are necessary to lead an abundant life. I had to show and give myself gratitude and you know what, I am grateful for you. Yes, that is right! I'm grateful that you decided to take a step of faith into tapping into your greatness and rediscovering your purpose in life. You are valuable to the world!

Philippians 2: 12-13 (MSG)
"What I'm getting at, friends, is that you should simply keep on doing what you've done from the beginning. When I was living among you, you lived in responsive obedience. Now that I'm separated from you, keep it up. Better yet, redouble your efforts. Be energetic in your life of salvation, reverent and sensitive before God. That energy is God's energy, an energy deep within you, God himself willing and working at what will give him the most pleasure."

When you go inward that is when the true discovery of self begins, and enlightenment of God increases. You begin to walk in your purpose. There is greatness inside of you. Having a Personal Relationship with God requires you to go inward. You must be willing to go inward to discover peace. No matter what comes your way, you must understand that you have the power inside of you to grow and seek change. Trials, tribulations, and setbacks will come, but you must continue to push in your faith and seek peace. What you do today impacts your tomorrow, therefore creates your future. Don't limit your thinking. Understand that there is a process. It is all about maintaining a positive perspective that will transcend to positive action.

The world is filled with trauma, war, and disappointment. This is the world we live in. But this is not the world we create within ourselves. This is not the world we create in our home. There has to be a balance. It is good to know what's going on but you must have awareness. You must be willing to go inward and self-reflect on how you can show up for yourself, your family, and your community. Having a grassroots foundation allows for you to understand the greater need of work that needs to be facilitated in ourselves and the community. Therefore, will create a change that is all productive and consistent. We must continue to thank God for the journey.

When we tell God "Thank you," we are expressing **Gratitude**. When we tell and show God **Respect,** we are saying that we trust God and we know that God has our best interest. We revere God. When we are mindful of these two practices God then provides us with **Encouragement** to keep us moving on the journey and purpose that was intentionally designed for our lives. Therefore, that shifts our mindset and actions towards **Appreciation** for all that God has done for us. Appreciation efforts are connected to not only what we say but all that we do. We can tell God how much we appreciate what he does but it's about our daily actions and interactions with others. Yes, this does require us to be intentional with our time daily. Time is essential for effective growth. God wants us to devote one on one **Time** with him.

When you are intentional about the personal time you spend with God, you are able to grow and see what is in store for your life. Trust that God has placed greatness inside of you, and therefore, you have the ability to share the greatness with others. Life is too short for "What ifs" and "I wish!" You have the power within to make a change. When you make intentional changes, it will produce fruitful growth that will transcend into other areas of your life. The time is now to take action! Don't limit your greatness!

Remind yourself that there is nothing too hard for God. Do you remember a time when your heart was heavy, and you prayed to God for guidance, strength, and clarity? You trusted God to answer that prayer and God did! He is the same God as yesterday. He is a God that is always on time. We must continue to seek God daily. Faith means that we have a *Favorable Abundance Increasing Through Him*. When we seek God daily with an open heart, mind, body, and spirit, our faith in God increases and we are gaining abundance in our life. It is an amazing feeling when you are able to shift your perspective, increase your personal skill-set, embrace something new, and take a chance on greatness. Your life will begin to understand the importance of having an impactful conversation while showing greatness at the same time, understanding that the conversations had to happen. As I grow and understand more about the importance of personal growth and intentional prayer, I am able to use it with those who are near to me, need confirmation, or a good word of greatness.

The world can be so cruel, and times will be hard. Trials and tribulations will come, hurt, grief, pain, drama, and ups and downs will happen, but isn't it good to know that God is true to helping and guiding us along the way. Isn't it good to know that God has given us the tools and everything we need to be great and to offer greatness to others? In other words, we as a society must understand the importance of shifting and balance. God is Great! We serve a great God. When we take the time to let the spirit guide us and open our heart, mind, and soul to Him, things will start to shift, and you will begin to see more of how much God is invested in you and how much He loves you. God is omnipotent, omnipresent, and omniscient. Nothing is too hard for God.

Life is too short, and we should want to live life to the fullest. Don't limit your thinking. Don't confine your mind to a box. Be willing to open the box-- your mind-- to explore and see what is inside of you. Don't let society define you or let people put limitations on you. Give back to others and God will give back to you. Show greatness and give greatness even at times when it is hard for you to forgive. Especially the ones closest to you. We must start with ourselves, family, and community.

Greatness is already inside of us. We have to just look around us, see, and hear. Think about what God did in the book of Genesis: He created the world. That is greatness! So, since we know that God did that, what makes you think that God didn't place greatness inside of you? Open your box--mind, heart, and spirit-- and slide the lid back an inch. Heck, even a centimeter to truly discover your true calling and growth. There are no limits to what you can achieve with your greatness and with God on your side, you can change your inner space to enlightenment and encouragement to greatness. Now, go out and BE great!

"Let Your Light Shine"

Matthew 5:13-16 (NIV)
"You are the salt of the earth. But if the salt loses its saltiness, how can it be made salty again? It is no longer good for anything, except to be thrown out and trampled underfoot. You are the light of the world. A town built on a hill cannot be hidden. Neither do people light a lamp and put it under a bowl. Instead, they put it on its stand, and it gives light to everyone in the house. In the same way, let your light shine before others, so that they may see your good deed and glorify your Father in heaven."

Glossary

Flow: a smooth uninterrupted movement or progress.

Gifts: a notable capacity, talent, or endowment.

Mantra: is a syllable, word, or phrase that is repeated during meditation.

Meditation: to engage in mental exercise (such as concentration on one's breathing or repetition of a mantra) for the purpose of reaching a heightened level of spiritual awareness.

Miracles: a divinely natural phenomenon experienced humanly as the fulfilment of spiritual law.

Prayer: an address (such as a petition) to God.

Release: to relieve from something that confines, burdens, or oppresses.

Talents: the natural endowments of a person.

References

Bible Gateway The Message (MSG). (2021, September 26). Retrieved from https://www.biblegateway.com/versions/Message-MSG-Bible/

Bible Gateway New International Version (NIV). (2021, September 26). Retrieved from https://www.biblegateway.com/versions/New-International-Version-NIV-Bible/

Healthline. 7 Ways Your Body Benefits from Lemon Water. (2021, February 26). Retrieved from https://www.healthline.com/health/food-nutrition/benefits-of-lemon-water#hydration

Merriam-Webster.com Merriam-Webster, 2021. Web. (2021, February 26). Retrieved from https://www.merriam-webster.com/

Mindworks Team. What is Mantra Meditation? (2021, September 26). Retrieved from https://mindworks.org/blog/what-is-mantra-meditation/

New International Version (NIV) Bible

Russell, Chris. (2019, February 13). Hawk Vineyard and Winery. Retrieved from https://www.2hawk.wine/2019/02/13/how-does-wine-fermentation-work/

The Glossary of Educational Reform. Growth Mindset. Great Schools Partnerships, 2013. Retrieved from https://www.edglossary.org/growth-mindset/

About the Author

Dr. Angel Jackson was born in Fort Riley, Kansas, and raised in Jeffersonville, Indiana. At the age of nineteen, she was called into the ministry and pursued God's purpose for her life. Dr. Jackson is an author, licensed, and ordained minister who provides opportunities for others to look inward to discover their greatness through her transformational writing and speaking. She is the author of the book, *The Power of Change: Understanding Your Resilience in the Midst of Growth* (2019). Dr. Jackson believes it is a gift to serve others in her community. Throughout her journey, she has helped many as the co-founder of *The Healing Tent* and as an Assistant Principal. In her day-to-day efforts, she is spreading love and light to others through her inspirational videos and podcast. Dr. Jackson lives in Southern Indiana with her husband, Brandon, and their two children, Emerald and Braxton.

To contact Dr. Angel Jackson, please send an email to:
dr.angeljackson1985@gmail.com

The Healing Tent Official Website and The Healing Tent Podcast
https://www.thehealingtent.org

Follow me on social media for Energy Shifting Tool Videos!
YouTube: Dr. Angel Jackson
Facebook: Angel Jackson
Instagram: iamdrjackson
Twitter: @iamdrjackson

www.ingramcontent.com/pod-product-compliance
Lightning Source LLC
Chambersburg PA
CBHW072021290426
44109CB00018B/2300